MISSING

Those who disappear

John Townsend

Published in association with The Basic Skills Agency

Hodder & Stoughton

A MEMBER OF THE HODDER HEADLINE GROUP

Acknowledgements
Cover artwork: Fred Van Deelan
Illustration: Josephine Blake
Photos: p. 6 © Mary Evans Picture Library; pp. 13, 16, 27 © Corbis; p. 24 © PA Photos.

Orders: please contact Bookpoint Ltd, 130 Milton Park, Abingdon, Oxon OX14 4SB. Telephone: (44) 01235 827720, Fax: (44) 01235 400454. Lines are open from 9.00 – 6.00, Monday to Saturday, with a 24 hour message answering service. Email address: orders@bookpoint.co.uk

British Library Cataloguing in Publication Data
A catalogue record for this title is available from The British Library

ISBN 0 340 84867 7

First published 2002

Impression number	10 9 8 7 6 5 4 3 2 1
Year	2007 2006 2005 2004 2003 2002

Typeset by SX Composing DTP, Rayleigh, Essex.
Printed in Great Britain for Hodder & Stoughton Educational, a division of Hodder Headline Plc, 338 Euston Road, London NW1 3BH by The Bath Press Ltd.

Contents

MISSING
HAVE YOU SEEN
THIS BOY ?

1 Did You Know?

Hundreds of people disappear every year.
Never to be seen again.
One minute they're sitting at home
or doing a job.
The next minute they've gone.
Disappeared into thin air.
Police files are full of such cases.
Strange cases.
All with the same title: **Missing**.

Many stories tell of people who just seem
to vanish into nowhere.
Gone.

- A husband went to buy a paper from the corner shop.
  He never arrived.
  His dog came back without him.
- A wife went to the supermarket in her new car.
  It was never found. Neither was she.
- A child rode into town to get an ice-cream.
  Two days later they found the bike in a field.
  Years later there was still no news.
  Not a sign. Nothing.

How can such things happen?
People give all sorts of answers.
Some reasons seem crazy.
Aliens? UFOs (Unidentified Flying Objects)?
Black holes?

Other ideas are more likely:

- kidnap
- murder
- running away
- loss of memory
- falling into a hole, into water or the sea
- getting lost
- suicide (or fake suicide).

Many websites claim to trace missing people.
You can pay to find a long-lost friend or loved one.
It seems that people 'disappear' all the time.
Most have a reason. There's no mystery.
But now and again someone leaves without trace.
Their police file has the label:
FOR NO APPARENT REASON.

Some mysteries of missing people
are years old now.
Who knows what happened to them?
Police files are kept open – never to be solved.
We may never know the truth.
And there's a question that we all want
to know the answer to.
Who will be next to vanish into thin air?

Here are some true stories that have puzzled
the world for years.
They tell of some of the most
famous MISSING people
and how they may have met their fate.

2 Lost at Sea

Some of the best-known mysteries happen at sea.
Many happen in the Bermuda Triangle,
which is an area between Florida,
the Bahamas and Cuba.
Some say that well over 1000 people
have vanished in this area over the last 50 years.
Ships and planes have just disappeared
without a trace.

However, perhaps the best-known mystery
was a long way from the Bermuda Triangle.
The strange story of the Mary Celeste
is known all over the world.
No one will ever know the real truth about it.

The ship set sail from New York in 1872
for just another trip across the Atlantic.
Captain Briggs, his wife, and
two year-old daughter were on board,
as well as a crew of seven men.

No one was ever seen again.
The Mary Celeste was found drifting
a few days later.
Not a soul was on board and it looked
as though the crew had left in a hurry.
The cargo of barrels was in place,
the ship's papers had gone
and much of the ship was wet through.
There had been heavy rain just a few days before.
The life-boat was missing
and a rope hung over the side.
Everything else was left in place
with no sign of any struggle.
But ten people and a life-boat had vanished . . .
for no apparent reason.

Just why would the Captain leave his ship?
What made them all leave in such a hurry?
Captain Briggs was known to be a good sailor.
He would never abandon a perfectly fine ship.
He certainly wouldn't risk the lives
of his wife and baby.
Nothing in the ship's log gave a clue of anything
unusual having happened.
But something made them leave.
What was it?

The Mary Celeste

What some people think:

- Illness. But why would they all need to get off the ship at once?
- A fight broke out. But there was no sign of blood or a struggle. Why would they all need to leave?
- Pirates. Nothing was stolen or out of place – not that this was the time or place for pirates!

- Storm, tidal wave or earthquake.
  Did they all fear the ship was
  about to be swamped?
  But wouldn't they be in more danger
  in a tiny life-boat?
- Was the ship about to blow up?
  Perhaps they thought the fumes from
  the barrels of alcohol were going to explode.
  But the cargo was all in place
  with nothing odd about it.

For some reason the crew left thc ship.
For some reason the life-boat
was never seen again.
Did it sink?
Did they land on an island and die of thirst?
And what about sea-monsters, sharks or even aliens?
You can find out more at:
www.maryceleste.net/

3 The Ellen Austin Story

Less than ten years after
the Mary Celeste mystery,
another crew went missing.
This time it was just south of Bermuda –
in the Bermuda Triangle.

The crew of the Ellen Austin saw a ship
drifting across the sea.
Captain Gould watched its sails flapping
and its masts swaying.
He lowered a rowing boat
and sent some men to take a look.

As they climbed aboard the silent ship,
the six men listened for signs of life.
Nothing. The splashing of the waves,
the creaking of the mast and the flapping of the sails
were all they could hear.
Both life-boats were still on deck.

Below decks, all was deathly still.
Nothing was out of place. Not a soul was on board.
It was like a ghost ship.
The six men were told to stay on board
and sail safely to the nearest port.
It would take a few days to reach land . . .
or so they thought.

The two ships set sail together.
But as night fell, so did an eerie mist.
Before long, the ships were hidden in thick fog.
Captain Gould lost sight of the other ship
as they sailed on through the dense fog.

When daylight came, the fog slowly lifted.
Captain Gould looked from one side of his ship
to the other.
There was empty ocean as far as the eye could see.
The ghost ship had gone.
It was never seen again – and neither were
the six men.

The story, with all its mystery and legend,
became yet another of the sea's dark secrets.
The fate of the missing men in the mist
remains unknown.

4 The Missing Baby

In the USA in the 1930s, a big story hit the news.
It sent a shock wave across the world.
A rich and famous family met with a cruel mystery.
Some called it the crime of the century.

Charles Lindbergh was a hero.
He was the first man to fly a plane
alone across the Atlantic in 1927.
America loved him. They called him Lucky Lindy.
When he married his millionaire bride,
the papers were full of his story.
They were stars.

The Lindberghs' first baby was in the papers, too.
On the night of 1st March 1932,
a ladder reached up to the baby's window.
A kidnapper crept into the room
where the baby slept in his cot.
No one saw the 20 month-old baby again.
A note told his parents to pay $50,000.

The world was shocked.
Everyone searched for the missing baby.
The police looked high and low.
Charles Lindbergh paid the $50,000
but nothing happened.
Two months later they found
a dead baby in nearby woods.
A man was arrested and found guilty of murder.
He was put to death in 1936.

But many think the man was not guilty.
Some think the whole trial was a cover-up.
Others say the kidnap story was just a hoax
to hide a killer in the family.

The police were never sure
about the body they found in the woods.
It was hard to tell who it really was.
In fact, it was bigger than the missing baby.
Many people think the real baby grew up
and is alive today.
Some people claim to be him!

Who knows what really happened?
The case of the missing baby remains
one of the great crime stories of the last century.

5 The Glenn Miller Mystery

The man with the famous big band
was a great hit in the 1940s.
Glenn Miller was a war-time star –
the first man to sell a million records.
He took his band around the world
to play for the troops.
'In the Mood' was a big hit
with his millions of fans.

After a visit to the UK in 1944,
Glenn Miller suddenly went missing.
He was never seen again.
There was no trace of his small plane
that left England on 14th December 1944.
It took off and flew out over the Channel
on its way to France.
It never arrived.
No one really knows what happened.

Glen Miller.

Some say the plane just crashed into the sea.
Others say it was shot down.
Some think an RAF (Royal Air Force) plane
dumped its bombs into the sea
and blasted Glenn Miller out of the sky.
Many other rumours spread.
People said they saw him later in France.
Did he go into hiding for some reason?
Was it all a plot? Was he kidnapped?
Did he know secrets?

Although his music lives on,
the live 'Glenn Miller sound'
was missed by millions.
Whatever happened that night,
one of the stars of the big band was lost.
And the mystery lives on.

6 What Happened to Lord Lucan?

The police never found Lord Lucan.
Some have been looking for him for 25 years,
all over the world.
Is he dead or did he get away to start a new life?
He became the most famous missing person
of the late twentieth century.

Lord Lucan lived in London
with his wife and three children.
Sandra was the children's nanny.
But it wasn't a happy house.
There were money problems and rows.
Lucan spent all his time gambling at his club.
The Lucans' marriage was over.
But on a November night in 1974,
their lives hit the news. Murder struck.
All the papers were full of the story.

Lord Lucan on his wedding day.

A 29 YEAR-OLD nanny's body has been found in a canvas tent bag in the basement of the Lucan's home in London. Lady Lucan discovered the body last night. She had head injuries and ran out into the street shouting 'Murder'. Police are trying to trace Lord Lucan.

Lady Lucan told the police how
her husband ran into her room in shock.
He was covered in blood and started hitting her.
She got away and raised the alarm.
By the time help came, Lucan had fled.
The police began a man-hunt for Lucan straight away.
Their nanny's killer had waited
in the dark basement, ready to strike.
When she came in to switch on the light,
a lump of pipe cracked down on her skull.

The nanny was due to be out that night.
But she changed her mind.
Did Lucan lay in wait to kill his wife . . .
and get the wrong woman?
She was the same size as his wife.
Who could tell them apart in the dark?
The police thought he did it.

Why else did he run from the murder scene,
never to be seen again?

Police found Lord Lucan's blood-stained car
in Newhaven – near the sea.
Did he escape on a ferry?
Did he get away in a speedboat?
The search began.
Many who knew him said he could never leave
his children or live in another country.
Some said he must have killed himself.
Perhaps he jumped off a boat
to drown all his worries.
Did he walk up into the woods
on the hills and shoot himself?
But his body has never been found.

There were all sorts of reports in the papers.
Some said Lord Lucan was seen in other countries.
Just a few years ago a headline said:
'IS LORD LUCAN ALIVE IN AUSTRALIA?'
Someone was sure they met him in Perth.
He would now be nearly 70.
A few years ago they wrote on his police file: DEAD.
But no one really knows.
Some think he might still come back one day.

7 Still Looking for Ben

Ben was just 21 months old when he vanished.
He hasn't been seen since 1991.
He was playing in a garden
on the Greek island of Kos.
A few minutes later he had gone.
No one knows where.
Today he would be in his teens.
But what happened?

The Needham family left England to live in Greece.
Their new home was among
the trees and lanes of Kos.
Eddie and Christine Needham would watch
their grandson play in the garden.
Ben was happy with his toys in the sun.
But one day when they called him indoors,
the garden was empty. Nothing.
They looked in the bushes.

They looked up and down the lane.
They searched the scrub all round the house.
There was no sign of little Ben
with his blond hair and big smile.

The days went by with no news.
The police couldn't find him.
Did a gypsy grab him and sell him?
Is he still alive?
His family will never give up hope.
They now live in England.
But they keep going back to search.

There is a reward if
anyone finds Ben.
Every year people say they see him
or know where he is.
But so far, all the reports have led nowhere.
The family's torture never ends.
They cling to the belief that someone out there
must know the truth.
But who?

8 Lost and Found

Some people go missing just for a short time.
They simply get lost. Some find help just in time.
But how many people get lost never to be found?
How many people are out there right now –
lost or stuck, or waiting for help?

John Johnson was 69 years old when he went
into the woods to collect a few logs.
It was 1998 in North Dakota, USA.
He walked too far into the woods
and lost his way.
It took him eight days to find his way out.
His family thought he had vanished into thin air.
John ate roots of lily pads to keep alive.
At last he found a road
and waited for a car to come along.
If he hadn't found the road,
he would have vanished forever.

Also in 1998, Li and her four friends got lost
in a cave in south west China.
It was pitch black when their candle blew out.
There was no food.
Day after day they waited for help.
Li's friends slowly died, but she clung on to life.
She was found at last.
The search party pulled her up into daylight
She had been missing for 42 days.
But she survived and came off the MISSING file.
Only just.

How many people disappear
by falling down a hole?
It happens from time to time.
But how many get out again?
In May 2001, a 26 year-old student went
down an old mine shaft in Somerset.
Matthew let himself down on a rope but fell,
pulling the rope with him.
He landed on a ledge about 15 metres down.

It was dark, damp and cold.
All he could do was wait.
Day after day in the wet.
He lost all sense of time.
There was nothing he could do.
Would he die and disappear without trace?
Who would know what happened?

After 11 days of just lying there,
waiting and fearing the worst, Matthew heard voices.
Would he get out after all?
Some children heard his cries.
It took three hours to get Matthew out of the hole.
They took him to hospital
and he was soon well again.
If those children hadn't come by,
no one would have known the truth.
Matthew would have been another student
who just vanished in mystery . . .
never to be seen again.

A cave rescuer, by the mine shaft where Matthew went missing.

9 The Biggest Horse Mystery

You may think that a horse is a bit big to go missing.
But one did do a vanishing trick
and no one really knows where he went.
The Shergar mystery may never be solved.
Just where did he go?

Shergar was a star.
He won the Derby in 1981
and he was the talk of the racing world.
He was worth a fortune.
But then it all changed.
Just before 9.00 p.m. on Tuesday 8th February 1983,
masked men took Shergar
from his stable at gun-point.
They also took away his groom
but let him go four hours later.

The thieves wanted £2 million.
But many people owned Shergar.
It took a long time for them all to agree what to do.
The thieves put up their price to £5 million.
The police thought it was the work of the IRA.

Then it all went quiet.
Nothing was heard again.
Was Shergar killed?
Was he let loose in a field in Ireland?
No one really knew.
Now and again someone said they saw him.
A skull was dug up and
everyone said it was Shergar.
Tests later proved it wasn't.

But people keep on looking.
One day they might find the truth.
Until then, Shergar is known for one thing.
Not for being a great racehorse.
But for going missing.

Shergar the racehorse.

10 And Finally . . .

Michael Kirby left Ireland to see his sister in London.
But he never arrived and no one knew where he went.
The police found a body in the River Thames.
His cousin came to look at the body.
Yes, it was Michael. So he said.

The body was taken back to Ireland for the funeral.
Four months later, Michael's daughter went
to London. In the middle of Victoria Station
she had the shock of her life.
She bumped into her father!
Michael was alive and well.
He had lost his memory and was living in
a hostel in London. So he wasn't dead after all.

So who did they bury instead?
No one knows. Just another one of the hundreds
of people who vanish every day.
Just another soul with the label: **Missing**.
But the question still remains . . .
Who will be next?